# PITFALL:
# WATER IN THE WILDERNESS

Gwendolyn Yarbrough

We want to hear from you. Please send your comments about this book to shapedforpurpose@gmail.com or visit www.gwendolynyarbrough.com

Thank you.

Pitfall

# Table of Contents

Chapter 1: Transitioning

Chapter 2: One Night Stand

Chapter 3: Tempo of Love

Chapter 4: On the Edge

Chapter 5: Desolate Place

Chapter 6: The Flow of Things

Chapter 7: Running on Fumes

Chapter 8: I'm Thirsty

Chapter 9: Order, Oil and Yet no Overflow

Chapter 10: Just One Drop

Chapter 11: Fresh Manna

Chapter 12: Hear the Rain

Chapter 13: Don't Strike the Rock

Chapter 14: Yes & Amen

Water in the Wilderness

Acknowledgement

Dear Intrigued Reader,

I'm so grateful you are interested in quenching your thirst for something more than just a standard book of written thoughts. Get ready to explore my wilderness on a whole unique dimension from my personal experience to becoming more than a conqueror by using strategies to express poetic and prophetic freedom!

The chapters arose staged to tell a triumphant story; to encourage you in your dry place and motivate you to push, pray, and decree victory as you venture to your own promised land. Feel free to mentally take time to absorb each chapter by reading slowly, pausing when needed, or jotting down notes in the notes section of this book. As you can see, this is not your typical book. It's written to stand out and stand up, even if you are in a desolate place!

Your Freedom Warrior,

*Gwendolyn Yarbrough*

# Chapter 1: Transition

As I mentioned in Sanctified and Sexy: Shaped for Purpose, of the man God sent into my life for and on purpose.

For this place of transition was to bring to my attention, that the things I wanted as mentioned were now in my face, while I was in detention.

Those past conditions had me second-guessing God's decision and I prematurely entered a place now foreign but forgiven.

My eagerness to love and the rumble in my stomach wasn't a bug but a new memory of the awakening of love.

But wait, I thought I was numb and dead to such until this man showed up making my heart thump.

I spoke to myself and believed it was just a fairy tale until I gave him my heart before he got down on one knee.

Saying to myself Oh well...

Yes, that hello Miss Lady he spoke so sweetly, made me realize that God heard my plea

but how could this be because my ex-husband was still haunting me.

Now playing a game of tug of war I see Mississippi came prepared, but the battle hasn't begun,

I thought we were just hooking up for fun.

But his demeanor let me know he wasn't about those games, and it was I he chose to one day have his last name.

I embraced the demand and at once agreed with his words that I was his girl, and he was my man.

Thanks to a mutual friend this new guy was becoming my new best friend.

## Chapter 2: One Night Stand

The warm spring day turned out to last longer than a night,

When he asked me for my number,

I was excited but thought to myself, yes right. But to my surprise what he said earlier,

 It was indeed no joke because he called me at once and that action almost made me choke.

 Is this real? Where did this guy come from?

I am a lady with three babies, recently divorced, and not put together like most ladies I know.

But that wasn't his concern because he sent me a song weeks later letting me know he had been praying and hoping for someone like me,

But you see I was still a bit broken and not ready to commit to anyone, not even me.

Though I was crazy head-over-heels for him the first time we met,

I guess my own insecurities led me to fret.

I remember this day like yesterday shortly after I moved to Plano to start my life over

he sent me an unexpected text and it read, "Will you......... me?"

I replied, "No not yet."

He ended up calling me because it was like he made himself a bet,

that I would say yes but I didn't want to be hurt again and he responded not by me and don't ever forget.

# Chapter 3: Tempo of Love

He had me at hello, but I had to remind myself to pace it and go slow

being we had already pressed fast forward going with the flow.

On his third visit to Texas, he spoke the phrase and boy oh boy did that put me in a daze.

Being that I spoke it on day three of speaking to him I had the good feeling he was the one for me.

I hated when he had to leave because it was like disbelief,

but he always would visit at the right time just before my head got hazy in my mind making me feel crazy.

It was so amazing how he would pop up

but I knew he was coming because I would feel it in my gut.

I would say to myself, "he's on his way and I know he won't tell me,

That's why I am cleaning my house and, in a hurry, and I wasn't that blurry.

This pace went on for about 3 1/2 years and with life happenings coming I was starting to become weary thinking

Yes, this is a game I knew it I gave him all of me before I knew it.

While yet holding on to our love.

# Chapter 4: On Edge

Yes, there was a little trouble in paradise from time to time

because at one point he had me thinking "Dude you are already made up your mind."

But truth be told it was his loving that made me lose track of time caught up in him and nothing else was on my mind.

However, he will let me know babe just give me a little more time,

 It wouldn't be five or six years before I made up my mind.

he would always wine and dine me

and kept spending lots of time with me,

that would always calm me.

Trips to the Sip' Chi and OK made me feel close and good to be babe anyway.

Still on edge hoping and wishing he would ask me again, but I guess that was just dreaming.

# Chapter 5: Desolate Place

As things turned tragic and my father was slowly passing,

My boo made the decision to move to Texas and that I thought was a huge blessing.

Being that my children were gone from me for a season,

 I really needed him closer to me and that was a good reason.

Empty, scared, and desolate inside,

I soon later lost my biological father to cancer and that's when I convinced myself

Yep, I was so glad this man I love is now by my side.

Not one day passed that I wasn't embraced by the smile on his face.

Remember the temple of love is now moving at a quicker pace.

My emotions were unstable, but I am going to church saying and praying that God is able.

 In my pain, I wasn't thinking about now living in shame being that this man I still love hasn't given me his last name.

# Chapter 6: The Flow of Things

By the time I realized we were really shacking up, three years had passed, and I was mad at myself saying, "Yo what's up?'

But not verbally to him because of all the things he has sacrificed and given up when he packed up but now, I was really confused but not to the point of being used

because remember it was already discussed marriage, so why keep up the fuss?

Saying to myself, "He will come around." Thanksgiving and Christmas were always mapped out of whose house we would visit, and boy was I proud.

This man cooked, cleaned, and worked extremely hard too, who would complain instead of just playing the game?

Besides, we have officially picked up the pace.

Any day now is what I felt playing housewife and I thought I wouldn't regret it.

Then it dawned on me he doesn't attend church with me, "What's up with that?" but seeing what I witnessed in the church wasn't a big deal to me, "at least we keep it real.

# Chapter 7: Running on Fumes

Four years now living together, I look up
thinking to myself this was just my luck

but the one day after service he picks me up
and says babe let's go to Burlington and see
what's up.

To my surprise, an Angel was there,

when she approached him out of nowhere.

Asking, "If I was his wife over there?"

She called for me to come over and look
him in the eye and asked him one more time,
"Son, is she your wife?

and he replied yes, and I looked at him in his
eyes like Oh, yes?

And then the older woman replied, "She
might as well be since y'all live like it
anyway. Hurry up and make her your wife
because God wants to give you both
something but not until you get it right."

 I bucked my eyes and tears began to roll
down my face,

My prayers are being heard and answered and my silence has been working too. He gave her his word that he would do right by me. So, turn to the next chapter and see if he got on one knee.

# Chapter 8: I'm Thirsty

Nope! Not even hardly........

now I'm acting thirsty but not for him my heart was injured but not beyond repair

all because I didn't want to believe he wasn't ready to take it there.

His heart was now being exposed, so I went on my own to search and seek God,

and one day while in prayer, I heard God speak, "Focus on your boys, books, business, and leave George alone, I got him."

Still distracted by my situation,

I couldn't focus and this phase was now starting to lose traction.

Almost desperate and confused the man of my dreams is now singing the Blues,

every time I bring up the martial news,

Focus Gwen and shut up! Didn't God speak to you, girl?

You gonna mess up!

Just follow his instructions so you don't have to lose more time waiting to share your good news that I was now thirsty for You!

# Chapter 9: Order, Oil, and No Overflow Yet

Another year now has passed since we met the lady in Burlington

but my thirst has since shifted,

I was on a mission to seek God without religion.

I believe the church's New Year's theme; order oil and overflow will happen for me.

So, I chanted it every Sunday until it got into my heart not really understanding

what I was praying or saying,

I just knew at this point I was ready for a major change.

The church folks, friends, and family started to laugh because what I was hoping for still hadn't come to pass

but nevertheless, I kept my press to pursue after God and let him do the rest.

As time passed long, another year gone, I shifted to a new congregation singing the same song order oil, and no overflow yet.

# Chapter 10: Just One Drop

The prophetic word I received that day

Couldn't have come at a better time.

I was just about to give up and I ain't even lying.

You see I was being haunted in the church by the spirit of perversion,

trying to escape my home front madness church was the place I was supposed to be feeling sadness.

Judge, cast down and ostracized by so-called Christians who were half my size,

but God spoke words to me, and it shifted my heart to still expect God to do his part.

This pit was meant to tear me apart, leave me for dead but God spoke not so,

you shall live and speak your heart, for your mouth has been shut closed but open your mouth and give God a shout because He is about to raise you up; because you kept the faith and didn't give up.

That was the day, I felt just one drop, my soul was refreshed on another quest to find my God and let him do what he does best.

Thank you, Lord, for letting just one drop.

# Chapter 11: Fresh Manna

By this time, my spiritual life has shifted,

no longer concerned with the thing that I just mentioned,

for God was working on me, and as I began to pray more of my life was revealed.

Look, I was nowhere close to being healed and what kind of man wants a broken vessel?

For she can't fill his cup when he feels like giving up.

That's when it dawned on me to work on myself.

I shifted my membership just before I jumped ship and that's when my help showed up.

God began to refill my cup.

You see what I thought I was ready for,

I was being molded into becoming and the time wasn't near,

so, I stayed faithful to the church so I could hear.

Yes! Hear clear concerning my next instructions and get off the path of self-destruction.

This by far was the best shift because God had now begun my reason to thrust,

Past my situation and in him put my total trust.

True enough fresh manna came into my life and that's when I discovered how to pray to be a purpose wife without shame, guilt, or strife.

# Chapter 12: I Hear the Rain

The cloud of hope, now hovered over my home,

favor like no other consumed my life and that is when I knew I was just now starting to do what was right.

This relationship pushed me closer to Christ, wanting Him more in my life, and slowed down trying to hurry up just to become his wife.

Therefore, I couldn't give up while in the pit of shacking contentment because it was this very situation that God used to make me look up.

Yeah, I was judged, rebuked, and set aside but my faith in God,

wouldn't let me die.

How has this church girl gone wild, still showing up in God's house with a praise and a smile?

I responded, "You will see after a while."

The rain was cleansing my heart, renewing my soul, and giving me good new goals to serve my Father in heaven.

My heart no longer was cold. This wilderness birthed my relationship with God, and who cares if he proposed or not.

# Chapter 13: Don't Strike the Rock

By now I have recommitted my life to Christ let's get back to the beginning this is your 6 1/2 by now I'm fed up with shacking.

Wondering aloud man how much longer do you think this is gonna last?

I know my worth and God knew me before birth and there isn't anything on this earth that will make me doubt him or cause me to lose my crown.

So, make up your mind.

You are running out of time, for I was now on a new mission to serve my God with clean hands and a pure heart.

Which made shacking extremely hard.

But the funny thing is, while I was fussing with him;

God spoke to my heart and said, "I have need of him don't strike the rock."

I was like whoa God what am I supposed to do now because at this point in my life I just want to please you.

God said, "stand still my daughter, your time is not in vain. In time, you will gain, just get out of my way and continue to obey. Shut your mouth and watch me make a way."

It took me a minute to grasp what I heard but peace calmed my nerves.

Therefore, I continued to serve.

# Chapter 14: Yes & Amen

I focused on God more and the things He had instructed me to do before,

 I grew to love His presence even more.

Things that used to bother me didn't anymore,

for I was confident in the promises of God and that was worth much more.

And here we are at the end of 2018, and he lives with me no more, but I still have my peace and joy.

 I still love him with all my heart because when I met him in '08, I knew now just like before,

But I quickly concluded that the call isn't on me,

If he wants me, I must do more.

One thing is for sure, when God makes you, a promise is guaranteed because what He has written by my name is just for me.

I'm hopeful to know, I am molded into now a purpose wife.

No longer holding on to grief, anger or strife;

Entering my Canaan flowing with milk honey and abundant life.

There is nothing more rewarding than hearing God say, "you are now being rewarded. For you have now entered your season of new beginnings in Me and My promises are still yes and amen, My daughter and My friend."

# Water in the Wilderness

Reader, I want to convey this immensely powerful scripture, Isaiah 43:19, *Behold I will do a new thing; now it shall spring forth; shall you know it? I will even make a way in the wilderness, and rivers in the desert.*

If you do not remember anything else, bookmark this in your memory, that every wilderness is temporary and, in every desert, there is a river of hope, life, and rescue. God was saying to the children of Israel, get ready for your new season of peace joy and prosperity.

The same goes for you. It is going to happen so quickly and suddenly; you will not even know how it manifested. But if you follow the path of instructions that He will give you, God will quench your thirst to get you out of the pit with His word. This place will soon be called your *yesterday*! I found it to be amazing, and that place of shacking is where I discovered the voice of God. That place was truly my pitfall. However, I still realized that every stronghold or strong man spirit in comparison is the same. How? Because those who wish to get out and live in freedom must go through deliverance after the confession of freedom. Not condemnation or shame.

Never mind those who are seeing you from near or far. Before you know it, people will wonder how this or how that, but truthfully, I ask myself the same question. How God? How do you still love me in this dark place? Why God? Why are you still concerned about me in this desolate place? When God? When are you going to do with God? What now God? What is it for me to do now God? Can you God? Can you really make a way out of no way God? Where to from here God?

I can honestly say, when church folks, nosy folk, messy folk, and unlearned folk shun me; God was there all the time. Cultivating me into who He wanted me to be and become. All those questions were the enemy's ideal way of plaguing my mind into believing I was not worthy of God's grace or mercy? Despite it was ABBA's voice that spoke words of assurance to my heart although, I am with you <u>always.</u> It was those words that helped and hoped for me. It was His touch that healed every hurt or pain by attending church every Sunday.

Despite my situation, I continue to worship and praise him. I was able to do that because I was open and honest about me, when expressing myself to the Savior. And guess what? He made away and I overcame every one of my critics!

Keep in mind, I am sharing my story with you to help you better understand, that you too can break out and break free from any type of bondage. My experience allowed me to better understand and relate to those alike. Just to give you an overview, over the past ten years and ½ years, life has taught me to stand up for my desires, beliefs, and most of all myself. I always had an issue trying to please others, fit in, or wanting to feel and be accepted and the truth of the matter is, this pit was the best thing that could ever happen to me.

Why? Because it gave me the opportunity to learn, grow, and mature in the areas that needed to be strengthened and challenged during that season. I did not take a day for granted. In conjunction, when it came time for me to enter my new place both naturally and spiritually, I did not blame him for his indecisiveness to move forward and marry me, when I thought or felt he should have because, internally, I was not ready.

Although I have been married before, even that circumstance should not have happened, it did. It is one thing to be married just because and another to be joined by God.

As a Freedom Warrior, it is my goal to help you understand bondage, give you strategies on how to break free and encourage you to mature into your greatness. Are you ready to say goodbye to today's bondages and catapult into your new season of all things *new*?

I am so excited for you! As your Inspiration Cultivator/Freedom Warrior, let me first say, you are stronger than what you think, wiser than you thought and braver than you'll ever be! Why? Because you want it! So, grab a pen or pencil and a notepad and jot down some notes as you discover this new place called freedom! On the next few pages, you will learn the ABC 's concerning water in your wilderness.

# Part A: Understanding Bondage

What is bondage? Bondage, according to the online dictionary, is the state of being a slave. Therefore, in simple terms, it's a place where you are held captive. Bondage can occur voluntarily or involuntarily.

In my case, because I wasn't processing the idea of living together, I found myself voluntarily agreeing to living that lifestyle with the imprinted thought, we will be getting married soon.

Soon like within the following year. I didn't see any "harm" in living together. Here's a wholesome guy who decided to pack up and move two states over to be with the woman he had already claimed to be his wife long before living together. But to my surprise, after looking up six years later asking him and myself, what are we doing and when are we getting married? That was an eye-opening experience.

In comparison, this is what happens to those in bondage of being involved with drugs, sex, alcohol, gossiping, lying, bitterness and past traumas or etcetera. Is that place we want to dwell in forever? No! But it happens and when it happens, it is then called living in bondage.

But thanks, be unto God, which always causes us to triumph in Christ, and make it manifest the Savior of his knowledge by us in every place, according to 2 Corinthians 2:14.

Meaning, in that very place that has us captive, that very place that has a strong hold on our life, that very place that the adversary wants us to get comfortable in, that very place of helplessness, that is the place that he has caused us to triumph in Christ.

God gives us the victory through his knowledge of how to break free and break out! Isn't that good news? Yes, you are in some type of pit right now but guess what? You are coming out victorious! Why, because Christ did not come for the Saint; He came for the Sinner. You and me!

This, a type of bondage, you are entangled in right now, just know I understand and can relate, and God brought me out, clean me up and set me up for victory. He is going to do the same thing and more for you.

Yes, bondage is real and can be voluntary but have the mindset to escape out of it. Take control of that very thing you are enslaved to and embrace the truth that it has you now, but it won't have you later.

Fast forward, the other side of voluntary bondage is involuntary bondage. This bondage you did not ask for, go looking for it or wanted it to be a part of you but it found you. you might be asking the question, "what about a certain type of bondage that hasn't been mentioned, Inspirational Cultivator?"

Here is what I want you to understand, that it is not your fault, but freedom is still yours! No that your place of captivity has an exit door too. Know that justice is in Jesus, and they did not get away! Know that no matter what happens or who it involved you matter to God and this place has a testimony with your name written all over it. In the following pages, I will give you strategies on how to break free from both voluntary and involuntary bondage.

Lastly, understand bondage has no color, creed, denomination or identity other than chains, ropes and bars. Bond-"age" has an age and end. Understanding bondage of any type of pitfall was designed to keep us from walking into our wealthy place but it has no authority anymore. Once we acknowledge our truth about bondage, who and how it has us captive, that's when we discover true freedom.

As you continue to read, I pray the light of hope, confidence and faith shines in your dark pit. I believe God for and with you.

# Part B: Strategies to Break-free

Here is a place you might need to bookmark as you move forward into experiencing freedom. Oh, you thought you didn't need to put in any work? Sorry, yes you do regardless of how, when, what or why you ended up bound you must do the work to break free.

Work must be done on your part. I know. "I was like God really? Haven't I done enough by confessing it?" But no, that is not enough. God was like, now it is time to pick up the pace and get to my Canaan. Do you know what Canaan means? It means, promise or wealthy place. let me tell you this, since entering this new place, it has proven to be just that. Now on to the strategies of how to break free from any type of bondage. Just remember as you commit to breaking free and exiting your pit the easier the task at hand will become.

Below are just a few of the strategies that I can almost guarantee will cause you to walk in total freedom. And it is as follows:

1. Acknowledge every pit or form of bondage you are experiencing right now. For example: addiction, unpleasant habits, bad attitudes, shaking, lack of commitment issues and so forth or forms of bondage and pits.
2. Ask God to help you escape.
3. Pray the Lord's prayer every day.
4. Affirm your victory.
5. Drowned out in cancel the noise of the naysayers.
6. Remain focused on your deliverance.
7. Fasting is a MUST!
8. Listen and obey to the instructions of the Lord by learning to hear God's voice when he speaks.
9. celebrate your progress without needing validation from others.

Now that I have listed the strategies to help better guide you through the process of breaking free you have now birthed a place called new. Be confident! One should begin to put these steps into action; you will see the results of heaven.

# Part C: Prophetic Encouragement

Well, we have arrived at the conclusion of the matter! Now that you have read my testimony, receive the tools, knowledge and resources to achieve your breakout, here is where I just say, I am proud of you! Nothing is impossible for them to believe, according to scripture.

I honestly could say because of God's word, I have gained strength slash power, wisdom and understanding of how to live my best life in Christ. I would not be anything without his help, guidance and grace! Just know that no matter what your situation maybe, there is nothing too hard for God, no pit too deep and no valley too low that his Salvation can I reach you.

Just keep in mind, while you fight for your freedom, you are not alone nor are you the only one. Not that being the only one matters because it doesn't; however what matters is that you too can experience limitless triumphant victories.

Let me also encourage you to push when you don't feel like it, decree even when your lips refuse to part, and dance like David regardless of if you're in a room full of people.

I can remember while fighting for my freedom so bad, that when I entered the House of God, people was trying to figure out why I was running around the church by myself like I did as if I had lost my mind or wailing out a scream from my belly because I could literally feel me getting closer to my breakthrough.

People didn't matter. What mattered was my freedom. My time in worship mattered, my shout unto the heavens mattered. And my praise dance mattered. Me laying it all on the altar mattered. Me forgetting about everyone else in the room and focusing on my deliverance mattered. Me surrendering my heart and life to Christ mattered. Me rejoicing during what seemed defeat mattered. You catching my point?

Therefore, let this be your prophetic word, you will come out of this before you realize it. You will be a testimony and a force to be reckoned with in the spirit. Your latter shall be greater, and your new name is victory!

I come in the name of the Lord, I prophesy to every one of your pits to close and never return or open again. Every valley rises every mountain of the devil be now cast into the midst of the sea.

I prophesy, no devil in hell can prevail against the plan and the thoughts that the Lord said wrote or thought concerning you! I prophesy, that the half haven't been told and your enemies will testify, it was the Lord's doing!

I prophesy, that this very place will bring God glory! I prophecy, not only will you be amazed but in your amazement your family members to gain salvation from your life example! I prophesy, that every target against you is now broken and redirected back to the enemy that launched it as my eyes.

I prophesy, that every arrow be broken before it strikes you and every stone turns to sand before touching you. I prophesy, that every worker spoken over your life from childbirth to now is denounced, canceled, nullified, terminated in the realms of the spirit and destroyed by the fire of God!

I prophesy that every dark place is being brought to light in life is being resurrected. I prophesy, unto you this day you shall live and not die. I prophecy, the Spirit of the Holy ghost boldness be made manifest in your life right now! And it is so in Jesus' name and for His namesake, amen!

Now be strong and of good courage, God is ready for you! God bless and remember this place will soon be called no more! Welcome to NEW!

# NOTES

_____

_____

_____

_____

_____

_____

_____

_____

_____

_____

_____

_____

_____

_____

_____

_____

_____

_____

_____

_____

_____

_____

_____

Made in the USA
Middletown, DE
19 September 2024

60703028R00031